SHAZZAM!

Anyone who has ever dreamed of being a magician will find out just how to go about it in this book.

In *Shazzam!* a master magician describes thirty-five of his favorite tricks for you — first as the audience sees them, and then as they are really performed. The *Shazzam!* magician suggests the kind of talk you might use to entertain your audience and distract their attention from your tricks during a performance. At the end of the book is a handy list of programs you might plan to give.

All of the tricks are surprisingly easy to learn. If you follow the ten golden rules, you will soon be able to put on The Greatest Magic Show on Earth!

SHAZZAM!

Gyles Brandeth
Illustrated by Mike Jackson

Cover by Norman Nodel

Nutmeg Press

Original edition published in English under the title of
  The Beaver Book of Magic by the Hamlyn Publishing Group Limited
Published in United States by Nutmeg Press
  A Division of Shelley Graphics Ltd.
Special edition prepared for Watermill Press
ISBN 0-89943-001-5

Contents

Introduction 7

Ten golden rules 9

One-star tricks 16

Two-star tricks 33

Three-star tricks 49

P.S. 58

The Greatest Magic Show
  on Earth 60

Suggested programs 62

Introduction

When I am cast away on my lonely desert island, along with my eight records and my copy of the Bible and the complete works of William Shakespeare, I shall certainly take with me:

10 dimes

1 nickel

2 $1 bills

1 straw

1 dark-colored bottle

1 drinking glass

3 cups

1 wand

1 writing pad

1 hat

1 blindfold

1 pair of scissors

1 piece of string

1 piece of rope

1 small piece of cork

1 bottle of water

2 bracelets

4 matchboxes

1 rubber band

a few handkerchiefs

a few pencils

a table

a stool

a piece of black cloth

a long-sleeved jacket

a pair of pants or slacks

several silk handkerchiefs

   two red

   two white

   two blue

a pack of cards

Why? Simply because with all the items in this list I could perform all the tricks in this book—except those requiring an assistant, of course—and present the greatest magic show on earth!

Ten golden rules

Ten golden rules

1 Practice! Practice! Practice!

No one in the world can become a master magician overnight. It takes practice and lots of it. The more you practice, the better you will be. None of the tricks in this book require an incredible amount of practice, but they all need some. The One-star tricks are the easiest to perform and master. The Two-star tricks are not quite so easy, and the Three-star tricks will need to be worked on quite thoroughly.

At the beginning of the description of each trick you will find a list of the *Equipment* you need for the trick, followed by *The trick* itself. *The trick* shows you how the trick is "seen" from the audience's point of view. *The secret* tells you how the trick is done from the magician's point of view. Study this very, very carefully. Read *The secret* at least *twice* before you start to practice the trick and then practice the trick at least ten times before you show it to anyone. By then you should be really confident that you have mastered the trick.

The tricks involving sleight of hand — *Coining it, Dollar power, The wand and the handkerchief* – and the more spectacular tricks will need to be practiced a lot more often. If you try to perform them before you have really mastered them, you will only spoil them and show your audience that you are not a true magician.

2 Polish your patter

A magician's "patter" is what he or she says while performing a trick. The patter that goes with the description of each trick, in *The trick,* has been specially written just as if a real performance was taking place. You don't need to use the suggested patter, but you will probably find it handy while you are learning the trick. Of course you will want to develop your own style of patter. Keep it lively. Throw in as many good jokes as you like, particularly when you want to distract your audience!

3 Remember you're a showman

Above all, a magician is an entertainer. Never forget this fact. That's why your patter and your appearance are as important as your tricks. If you make your audience laugh, they will enjoy your magic that much more. And if you look the part — either because you're all dressed up as a wizard or because you're looking super magician-like — they will believe in your tricks more easily.

One other word about dressing up: a magician's hat is practically a must. It need not be a top hat, but you will need a hat with an inner lining. Check the descriptions for each trick. Your pockets and sleeves are part of the act too.

Be as confident as you can. Confidence will come with practice and experience. If you know you know your tricks, if you are sure all your props are in position, if you can see that you are looking the part, there is no need to be nervous. Nothing can go wrong. Don't rush your tricks, but at the same time keep the show moving.

4 Don't attempt the impossible

You might like to make rabbits appear out of hats and saw people in half, but only very experienced professional magicians with plenty of money can perform such elaborate tricks. One day, when you can afford the expensive equipment that more complicated tricks require, you can try throwing daggers and making a dozen doves appear out of nowhere. Meanwhile, stick to more straightforward magic. If properly performed, it can be as impressive to watch as the most elaborate tricks imaginable.

Most of the tricks in this book can be performed with props you find around the house. Rather than paint a stick (or dowel) black, you might want to buy a wand in a magic shop. Several tricks require "magic" handkerchiefs. You can use ordinary handkerchiefs, but you will find it well worth spending your pocket money on some professional magician's "silks." These can be bought from any good magic shop. They come in all colors and are useful because they can be squeezed into tiny balls and hidden easily.

And remember: just because the One-star tricks are the easiest to master, it doesn't mean that they won't thrill your audience. Often the simplest trick is the one that baffles the audience most. All the tricks in this book have been or are being used by professional magicians all around the world.

5 Use your experience

As a magician, you will want to improve your performance all the time. The more shows you give, the better they will get; the more practice you give to a trick, the more polished it will become. With experience, you will probably want to change the way you present some of your tricks. Begin by doing them exactly as they are described in the book. Later, when you are really at home with them, you can change them to suit yourself.

Some tricks, you will find, lead to other tricks. For example, once you have learned how to "palm" an object (as you will in *Coining it!* on page 53), you will be able to use "palming" in all sorts of marvelous tricks of your own.

6 Use your audience

An audience likes to feel involved so, whenever you can, invite a member of the audience forward to help you. The audience will be less suspicious of your tricks also. Always use a member of the audience to blindfold you (unless, of course, you need to be able to peep under the blindfold!) but never use the same member of the audience twice during the same show. If you do, the rest of the audience will think you have an accomplice, or secret helper. You will be using an accomplice in some of your tricks, but you don't want the audience to know that fact. Sometimes you will be using an assistant, and, of course, you let the audience know.

7 Learn to mislead your audience

The more interesting your patter and the busier your

hands, the less your audience will notice. You don't want your audience to see anything they're not supposed to see, so you must do all you can to *misdirect* them at important moments in your performance. Remember that the audience will look where you look. Remember that they will look at anything you point to. Remember that they will look at anything that's moving.

8 Keep your wits about you
There are lots of card tricks described in this book, but the best card trick of all isn't included here at all! You will

be amazed by how often, when you offer a pack of cards to a member of your audience and ask them to pick one, they accidentally let you catch sight of the card! It happens all the time. If you do happen to see the card, don't let on. Forget the trick you were going to perform and invent a new trick on the spot. It can be as clever as you like. It can *seem* impossible and, for once it can *be* impossible. You know the secret card and that's all that counts.

9 Plan your show

A good magic show needs a splendid opening trick, a fantastic closing trick and lots of color and variety in between. It should never be too long. If you want some idea of what combination of tricks works well, take a look at *The Greatest Magic Show on Earth* on page 60.

10 Never! Never!

Never perform the same trick twice in the same show. If you do your audience will begin to catch on to the way you do it. And *never, ever, EVER* tell anyone how any of your tricks are done!

One-star tricks

Silks from nowhere

Equipment: 2 silk handkerchiefs

The trick: My pockets are empty — and when I say *empty* I mean completely and utterly *empty*! Look: there's nothing in this one, and there's nothing in this one.

I've turned my pockets inside out to prove that they're empty, but if you all shout the mighty magic word *Shazzam!* something amazing may happen.

"Shazzam!"

No, my pockets are still empty. You'll have to shout louder than that.

"SHAZZAM!"

It's worked! Look at this beautiful red silk in my left pocket and this gorgeous blue one in my right pocket! They came from nowhere, thanks to you.

The secret: The silks didn't come from nowhere, of course — they came from inside your pockets. The audience didn't see where they were hidden when you turned your pockets inside out because there is what's called a "dead corner" in pants, or slacks, pockets where a small object can be safely tucked and remain unseen even when the linings are turned out.

A magician's silk is a very useful piece of equipment to have. It looks just like a large silk handkerchief, but it is made of a material that can be squashed into a small shape very easily. Before beginning this trick, simply tuck two tightly rolled-up silks into the dead corners of your pants pockets. When you need to get the silks, put your hands in your pockets and work the silks out of the corners with your thumbs. Then produce them with a grand gesture!

You can use the dead corners in your pockets for hiding all sorts of other small objects (coins and dollar bills, for example) and you can build up amazingly complicated routines around them.

Card sharp

Equipment: 1 pack of cards

The trick: To perform this trick I need the assistance of a member of the audience. Will you volunteer? Thank you very much, sir.

Now I would like you to take this pack of cards and cut it in two.

Now put aside the upper part of the pack.

Please count the remaining cards onto a pile on the table. Put them face downward, one card at a time.

Now remove the top card and the bottom card.

Here we've reached the tricky bit. Kindly pick up and study the card that is now at the top of the pile. Look at it carefully. Don't let me see it. But think about it. Concentrate hard.

Is your card a black card?

"It is."
Is your card an Ace?
"It is."
Is your card the Ace of Spades?
"It is!"

The secret: Before performing the trick you have checked to see what the next-to-the-bottom card in the pack is. In this case, it was the Ace of Spades. All you have to do now is remember the Ace of Spades.

Your victim begins by cutting the pack in two and discarding the top part. This doesn't change the position of the Ace of Spades. Then he counts out the remaining cards onto a pile on the table, which reverses their order. The Ace of Spades, having begun as the next-to-the-bottom card, is now the next-to-the-top card, so that when the top and bottom cards have been removed, the top card has to be the Ace of Spades.

The time you spend in discovering that the card *is* the Ace of Spades is just a lot of showmanship!

Hole in one

Equipment: 1 nickel
  1 piece of paper with a small
    round hole in it

The trick: Let's get on with the magical challenge! I have here a nickel and a piece of paper. In the middle of the piece of paper is a hole. As you can see the hole is just about the size of a dime.

Now what I would like to know is this: can anyone here pass the nickel through the tiny hole without tearing the paper? They can't. Well, watch me do it!

The secret: Unless a member of your audience already knows the secret — which is just possible, but most unlikely — not one of them will be able to pass the nickel through the hole without tearing the paper.

To perform the impossible yourself, you must fold the sheet of paper in two right through the center of the hole and then slide the coin inside the folded paper so that part of it shows through the hole.

Now pull the paper very gently downward and outward on both sides of the coin and watch how easily the coin slips through the hole.

The nine-card trick

Equipment: 9 cards

The trick: I'm going to lay nine cards out on the table, face upward like this.

Now I'm going to leave the room. While I'm out of the room I want you to choose one of the nine cards. When I return I will ask one of you to point to each of the cards in turn, and when that person points to the card you have chosen I will tell you.

The secret: When you come back into the room after the secret card has been chosen, the member of the audience who points to the cards is actually your accomplice. He or she will touch each card in a particular place and the place that is touched will indicate the secret card's position on the table. So if your accomplice touches all the cards in the top left-hand corner, you will know that the secret card is the one in the top left-hand corner of the lay-out, and if each card is touched right in the middle, you will know the card you want is in the center.

To make the trick a bit more baffling, you can arrange for your accomplice to touch the card in the position you need to know just once. If your accomplice shows you where the secret card is when pointing to the first card, all the other cards can be touched in different places and so help confuse even the most eagle-eyed member of the audience.

Coins in the hat

Equipment: 10 dimes, each one dated
a different year
1 hat
1 blindfold

The trick: I would like a member of the audience to step forward and assist me with this trick. Thank you, madam. Would you please begin by blindfolding me. Make quite sure that I can't see a thing.

Now you will see that on the table I have arranged ten coins. They are all dimes and each one belongs to a different year. What I would like you to do is to choose one coin. Now take that coin and pass it around the audience. Get everyone to look at it closely and memorize the date carefully.

Now bring the coin back to the table and put it and all the other coins into my top hat. Shake the hat a little so that the coins are all jumbled up. Now pass me the hat, but hold it up high. I will feel inside the hat and find your coin.

Here it is!

The secret: Before you perform this trick place all ten coins in the freezer compartment of a refrigerator. This will make them very cold, and they will stay cold even if you bring them into a warm room and don't use them right at the beginning of your performance.

The coin that the member of the audience chooses from the ten will be passed around and handled by lots of different people. Their handling of it will make it a lot warmer than the other nine coins, so that when you put your hand inside the hat all you have to do is feel each coin until you come to one that's warmer than the others. That's the coin you want. Now produce it from the hat and tell the audience its date!

Shapes shake-up

Equipment: 1 sheet of writing paper
1 pencil
1 hat
1 blindfold

The trick: I'm wearing a thick blindfold. I can't see a thing, and yet when I ask members of my audience to draw shapes onto slips of paper for me I will be able to tell them the shapes they have drawn! It sounds impossible. It *is* impossible. But I can do it!

Let me tear a piece off this sheet of writing paper and give it to a member of the audience. Now, sir, would you kindly draw a triangle onto your piece of paper, fold the paper in two, and place it inside my top hat.

Let me tear off another piece of writing paper and give it to someone else. Now, madam, would you kindly draw a circle onto the paper, fold it, and place it inside that hat.

Finally, let me give this last bit of paper to a third member of the audience. Now, sir, would you be so kind as to draw a square onto the paper, fold the paper and place it inside that hat.

Now all three folded pieces of paper are inside that hat. Would someone kindly hold the hat up so that all can see it. I will now pick out one of the pieces of paper and tell you what shape is drawn on it, even though I am totally blindfolded...It's the CIRCLE!

The secret: It's so simple, you'll be surprised when you hear how it's done! The first and third pieces of paper you tore off will both have one rough torn edge and three smooth edges. But the second piece will have *two* rough torn edges and two smooth edges.

Since you know that the circle was drawn on the second slip of paper and you also know that the second slip of paper has two rough edges, all you have to do is feel all three slips of paper inside the hat and pick out the one with two rough edges.

You can perform the same trick with any three drawings. You don't have to use a triangle, a circle, and a square. For example, you could ask the first and third members of the audience to draw a banana and pineapple on their slips of paper, and the second member of the audience to draw an apple on theirs. Then you would boast about the magic way you could always recognize an apple, even when wearing a blindfold.

To make the trick that much more mystifying, make a member of the audience tie the blindfold around you so that everyone is quite certain you can't see.

The rattling matchbox

Equipment: 4 matchboxes
1 coin

The trick: As you can see I have here three empty matchboxes. Would somebody from the audience kindly step forward and inspect the matchboxes. They really are empty, aren't they?

Now, sir, will you be so good as to lend me a coin. Thank you. Place the coin in one of the three matchboxes. Close all three matchboxes and line them up for me on the table.

Watch me closely while I shuffle the three matchboxes. Your coin is in this box isn't it? Yes, I can hear it rattling. Now let me shuffle the matchboxes again. Can you now find the matchbox containing the coin?

You're wrong! Your coin's in this one.

The secret: You have a fourth matchbox hidden up your sleeve! You keep it in place with a rubber band just above your wrist. The hidden matchbox also contains a coin.

When you shuffle the three matchboxes the first time, you deliberately pick up a matchbox you know to be empty and give it a shake. Although it is empty, the matchbox up your sleeve will rattle and your audience will think it is the matchbox you are holding that is rattling. This will fool the member of the audience who has got to choose the box containing the coin, so that when you shuffle all three boxes a second time, he is almost certain to pick up the empty box that he thought he heard rattling.

Hide and seek

Equipment: 3 cups
1 coin

The trick: On my table I have three cups and one coin. I'm going to leave the room and, while I am gone, I would like a member of my audience — any member at all — to step forward and hide the coin under one of the three cups.

When I return I will need absolute silence. No one is to say a thing or move a muscle. Any distraction could disturb my concentration. I want the room to be totally quiet and everyone to be completely calm.

I will then walk straight over to the table and pick up the very cup that is hiding the coin!

The secret: You have to have an accomplice who will sit with the audience. No one must know he or she is there to help you. When you come back into the room, your accomplice will be using a finger as a signal. If he or she is holding a finger on the middle of the mouth it means the coin is hidden under the middle cup.

If your accomplice is holding a finger to the left of his or her mouth it means the coin is hidden under the left-hand cup.

If your accomplice is holding a finger to the right of his or her mouth it means the coin is hidden under the right-hand cup.

If your accomplice is holding three fingers on the mouth it means the audience has tried to outsmart you and put coins under all three cups. If the fingers are nowhere near the mouth it means that the audience has tried to out-outsmart you and has not hidden the coins under the cups at all!

Change the Ace

Equipment: 3 cards

The trick: As you can see I have here three Aces: the Ace of Spades, the Ace of Diamonds, and the Ace of Clubs.

With your help I can change one of these Aces. Let me gather the three cards up, turn them over, and invite a member of the audience to blow on them. Well done!

Now I've got the Ace of Spades, the Ace of Clubs, and the *Ace of Hearts*!

The trick: The secret lies in the fact that you had the Ace of Hearts on you all the time! When you held up the three Aces at the beginning of the trick, you said the middle Ace was the Ace of Diamonds and your audience believed you because it looked like the Ace of Diamonds. If you hold the Ace of Spades and the Ace of Clubs, over the Ace of Hearts so that only the pointed part of the heart shows, the card will be mistaken for the Ace of Diamonds.

At the end of the trick you simply reveal the three cards to be what they are: the Ace of Spades, the Ace of Clubs, and the Ace of Hearts.

This is a very simple trick, bit if it is performed quickly it will fool your audience. It is an excellent trick to use right at the beginning of a routine of several card tricks.

Two-star tricks

The magic bracelet

Equipment: 1 piece of string
1 bracelet

The trick: I need two members of the audience to come up and assist me please.

Now what I would like you to do is to tie one end of this piece of string to my left wrist and the other end of the piece of string to my right wrist. Tie the string with as many knots as you like.

Here I have a simple bracelet. I would be grateful if you would inspect it. Thank you. Now hand it to me and kindly return to your seats.

I will now turn my back on you for ten seconds — and when I turn around again you will find that the bracelet has been threaded onto the string!

The secret: There's a second bracelet — identical to the first — and you've had it hidden up your sleeve all the time!

When you come on to perform this trick you have already hidden the secret bracelet up one of your sleeves. You have pushed it over your wrist and wedged it up your sleeve. When you turn your back on the audience you simply slip the bracelet they have seen into a pocket, reach up your sleeve, and pull down the secret bracelet!

When you have practiced this trick a few times you will feel confident enough to do it facing the audience with your hands and wrists covered with a black cloth. The audience will find that doubly impressive.

The mighty mind reader

Equipment: Several slips of paper
A few pencils
1 hat

The trick: Ladies and gentlemen, here are some blank slips of paper. I would like to give a slip to each of you.

Now would you be so kind as to write a two, three, or four word message on your slip of paper. The message can be about anything you like. When you have written your message, fold up the piece of paper so that no one can see what you have written. Now place your folded slips of paper inside my hat.

I will now proceed to amaze you with the mightiest example of mind reading you have ever witnessed. I will pick out a slip of paper, hold it to my forehead and tell you what is written on the slip of paper. I will do it with every folded paper in turn. When I have finished I would like any member of the audience whose message I have not read out to stand up. I guarantee that not one of you will stand up!

The secret: Before beginning this trick you have written a two, three, or four word message of your own on an extra slip of paper and hidden it inside the hat, tucked somewhere along the lining where no one will see it.

When you pick out the first slip of folded paper from the hat and press it to your forehead, you read out the message you have written on your hidden slip. You then open the slip you held to your forehead as if you are checking it, but in fact you are reading what your *next* message is going to be.

Working this way, each time you hold a slip of paper to your forehead the message you read out is, in fact, the message you read on the last piece of paper you looked at.

When you get to the last of the real messages, remove your own hidden slip of paper and hold it to your forehead while you announce the final message that was written by a member of the audience. You will then have told everyone their messages without appearing to have read any of them!

For this trick to be truly effective you need an audience of at least fifteen people. With fewer people, someone may notice that you announced one more message than there are members of the audience.

String so strong

Equipment: 1 piece of string
                    1 straw
                    1 pair of scissors

The trick: I have here a perfectly ordinary piece of string. Would you care to inspect it, madam?

And I have here a perfectly ordinary drinking straw. Now I will thread the string through the straw so that there is a piece of string hanging out of both ends of the straw.

Now I will bend the straw with the string in it and cut the string and the straw in two — like so!

You saw me cut it, didn't you? Now watch me blow on it.

I've blown on it, and I've mended it! Madam, would you please pull the string out of the straw and check that it is still in one piece just as it was when your first inspected it. The string is in one piece, but the straw is cut in two!

The secret: The secret lies in the straw, which you did *not* offer for inspection.

Before performing the trick you should make a neat cut about an inch long in the middle of the straw, so that when the straw is bent, with the cut on the inside, the string, if the ends are pulled, will come clear of the bend. You keep the exposed stretch of string hidden from the audience with your thumb and forefinger while you cut through the straw with the scissors.

Finally you hold the pieces of straw in your closed hand while you invite a member of the audience to pull the complete piece of string out of the straw. While the member of the audience is holding up the piece of string, you hold up the two pieces of straw and the rest of the audience bursts into thunderous applause!

Red, white, and blue

Equipment: 6 silks — two red, two white, and two blue

The trick: On my table I have three very attractive and very remarkable silk handkerchiefs: one red, one white, and one blue. In my pockets I have nothing at all — as you can see.

I am going to tie the red handkerchief to the blue handkerchief like this, and place them in my right-hand pocket. To make sure there's no cheating I'll let you see the end of the blue handkerchief at all times. I'll pull it slightly out of the pocket so you can keep an eye on it.

Now I will put the white handkerchief inside my left-hand pocket. And here comes the magic! I'm now going to send the white handkerchief from my left pocket to my right pocket — VOOMVOOMVOOM! It's done!

Watch me pull out the blue handkerchief from my right-hand pocket: the white handkerchief is tied to it now! Here they are: the red, the white, and the blue all tied together in a row!

The secret: You begin the trick with *six* silks, not three. You have two reds, two whites, and two blues. Before performing the trick tie one white silk between one red and one blue, roll them into a tight bundle and hide them in the dead corner of your right-hand pants, or slacks, pockets.

When you begin the trick you can show your audience the linings of both your pockets and they will think your pockets are empty. When you have tied the red and blue silks together and are seen to place them in your right-hand pocket, push them right into the pocket so that they are out of sight, saying, "To make sure there's no cheating, I'll let you see the end of the blue handkerchief at all times." You then pull out the blue end of the three handkerchiefs hidden in the dead corner of your pocket. With practice you will be able to do this as though it were all one movement, and your audience won't realize that the corner of blue handkerchief isn't the same handkerchief as the one they saw you put in your pocket.

Once you have put the white silk into your left pocket you can forget about it, though if you want to show that your left pocket is completely empty when you have shown the three handkerchiefs tied together, you can carefully move the white handkerchief into the left pocket's dead corner while your audience is applauding madly.

Indian rope trick

Equipment: 1 rope
1 bottle
1 small piece of cork

The trick: The trick I am about to show you is one of the oldest pieces of magic in the world. It has been performed by great Indian magicians for thousands of years.

Here I have a very old Indian medicine bottle, and here I have a short length of Indian rope. Watch me place the rope inside the bottle. Now watch me turn the bottle upside down. Whoops! The rope has fallen out. That's because I forgot to say the ancient Indian magic word. I'll say it now and we'll see what happens. PIN-DIPINDIDIRIPU!

Look, when I turn the bottle over, the rope stays where it is and — even more amazing — I can swing the bottle by the rope.

Now if you care to examine the bottle and the rope for yourselves, you will see that this trick can only be performed by a true magician.

The secret: Inside the bottle you have hidden a small piece of cork. When you turn the bottle upside down the first time, you are careful not to turn it right upside down. You just turn it enough for the rope to fall out. When you next turn the bottle upside down you do it properly, so that the small piece of cork gets stuck between the neck of the bottle and the rope. Now the rope won't fall out, and you can even swing the bottle with the rope.

When you want to remove the rope from the bottle turn it the right way up and push the rope down into the bottle. This will allow the cork to drop to the bottom of the bottle. Pass the rope to your audience for them to examine. While they are taking the rope from you, hold the bottle upside down with the mouth of the bottle in your palm. The piece of cork will fall into your hand, and you can then pass the bottle to the audience in safety.

You will need to practice with different sizes of bottle, rope, and cork before you get the trick just as you want it. A medicine bottle, or a bottle of dark-colored glass, is ideal. The width of the rope and the piece of cork together should be slightly greater than the opening of the neck of the bottle.

The wand and handkerchief

Equipment: 1 handkerchief
           1 wand

The trick: You see here my left fist. Watch me cover it with this handkerchief. Now watch me push the wand into my fist. It's pushing the handkerchief with it, as you can see.

It's a real fist, a solid wand, and a handkerchief without holes. Have a look if you don't believe me.

Now I'm going to push the wand right through the handkerchief, without breaking the wand or tearing the handkerchief! Here goes.

I've done it!

The secret: When you first demonstrate what you are going to do, make a slight well in the handkerchief that is over your fist by pushing the first two fingers of your right hand into your left fist. Make a big, dramatic gesture of this, so that everyone can see what you are doing. Then put one end of the wand into the well and push it down far enough so that the handkerchief begins to appear at the other end of your fist with the center of the handkerchief obviously on the end of the wand.

Once the audience has seen you do this give them the handkerchief and wand to inspect, and then start again. Again lay the large handkerchief over your left fist with the center of the handkerchief over the opening, and once more make a grand gesture of creating a small well with the first two fingers of your right hand. This time however, only one of your fingers goes inside your fist, and the other goes outside your left thumb. It is into this "well" that you poke your wand this time and, of course, it slips through without difficulty.

This is a very effective trick, but requires plenty of practice before it can be performed perfectly.

Read the pack!

Equipment: 1 pack of cards
1 blindfold

The trick: I am blindfolded. I cannot see with my eyes, but I can see with my incredible magician's mind!

Here I have a pack of cards. I will hold it out so that it faces you, and I will go through the pack telling you the name of each card in turn.

I got all fifty-two of them right, didn't I? And the pack was facing you all the time, and I was blindfolded. Unbelievable — and yet you saw it happen!

The secret: This fantastic trick has you fooling the audience twice. First, you can see under the bottom of the blindfold. But, more important, the real magic is in the way you present the pack of cards.

Before beginning the trick, hold the pack of cards face downward and turn the top card face upward. When you hold out the pack to face the audience, have this card facing them. They will think, very naturally, that this is actually the bottom card in the pack. As they are looking at the card, you name it for them, at the same time noting the card that is facing you, by peeping under the blindfold.

When you have named the first card, put the pack behind your back and transfer the card you have just glanced at to the "audience" side of the pack. Now show the pack to the audience, naming the card they can now see and noticing the new one that is facing you. Continue this until you have been right through the pack. You will know when you have named all fifty-two cards because all that will face you is the back of a card — the back of the card you first showed your audience.

The trick is amazing enough performed without a blindfold, but the blindfold makes it that extra bit special. It also makes it that bit trickier to perform.

Telepathy

Equipment: None

The trick: I'm going to need an assistant for this trick. Are there any volunteers? You, sir? Thank you very much. If you will step over here, I will explain to you what I would like you to do. Don't worry, it's very simple.

I am going to leave the room and, while I am out of the room, I want the rest of the audience to choose an object in the room. When I return I want you to name various objects in the room and when you have named the one the audience has chosen, I'll tell you. Okay?

(Five minutes later)

Well, here I am again. Has the audience chosen an object?

"They have."
Good. Now start giving me some ideas.
"Is it the fireplace?"
No.
"Is it the clock?"
No.
"Is it the ashtray?"
No.
"Is it the lamp?"
No.
"Is it the blinds?"
No.
"Is it the picture?"
No.
"Is it the rug?"
No.
"Is it the table?"
No.
"Is it the doorknob?"
Yes it is!

The secret: The assistant you invite to join you from the audience is, in fact, your accomplice. When your accomplice is asking you what you think the object is, just before the right object is mentioned an object that has four legs will be mentioned. As soon as your accomplice has mentioned an object with four legs, by asking, "Is it a chair?" or "Is it a table?" or "Is it the cat?" you know that the next object *must* be the one you're looking for. It always will be.

You can repeat this trick many times before the rest of the audience begins to suspect what's up, but it's probably best not to try it more than three times at the same performance.

Three-star tricks

The magic water

Equipment: 1 bottle of water
1 drinking glass
1 handkerchief

The trick: Ladies and gentlemen, I am about to turn the water in this bottle into magic water, water that will obey my every command! Let me say the magic word — WIBBLYWOBBLYWIBBLYWOO — and it's done!

Now I shall pour some of the magic water into this glass. Now I shall cover the glass of magic water with my handkerchief. And now I shall turn the glass upside down, but I will tell the magic water to stay where it is and not fall out.

Look, I've done it!

Now I am going to tell my glass of water, which is still upside down, to start to bubble and boil. Oh, Magic Water, begin to bubble and boil! Yes, it's beginning to bubble — you can even hear the bubbling!

The secret: When you fill the glass, only pour in enough water to make it three-quarters full. When you have covered the glass with the handkerchief, pick it up with your right hand and with your left hand draw the handkerchief's edges under the bottom of the glass. Hold the bottom of the glass and the handkerchief with your left hand and press down the center of the handkerchief with your right hand until it just (but only just) touches the water. Then, with a sharp twist of the wrist turn the tumbler over. Don't worry — the water *won't* fall out.

Now, still holding the tumbler upside down draw the handkerchief around the glass until it becomes tight and smooth across the rim of the glass. The water will now drop to this level (but no further) and a vacuum without air will have been created at the bottom of the glass. Gradually, air will seep through the handkerchief and travel through the water to fill the vacuum at the bottom of the glass. This will create the boiling and bubbling noises.

The zany zoo-keeper

Equipment: 4 Aces
4 Kings
4 Queens
4 Jacks

The trick: Once upon a time there was a zany zoo-keeper who had four lions, four tigers, four cheetahs, four leopards, and four empty cages. He decided to put a lion into each cage and, since for the purposes of this trick the lions will be the Aces, I will now put four Aces face upward on the table.

He decided to put a tiger into each cage as well, so I'll now put a King on top of each of the Aces.

He decided to put a cheetah into each cage, so I'll put a Queen on top of each King.

Finally, he decided to put a leopard inside every cage, which is why I'm putting a Jack on top of each Queen.

Unfortunately the animals all began to fight, and the zoo-keeper suddenly realized that he should have kept the different kinds of animals apart. Now I'll collect the four piles and invite a member of the audience to cut the pack face downward. Now I'll deal out the sixteen cards into four piles and when you turn the four piles over you will find that the Aces are all together, the

Kings are all together, the Queens are all together, and so are the Jacks!

The secret: This trick is one of the all-time "greats." It can't go wrong. It never fails — so long as you play your part properly. No magic is involved. The trick works automatically, provided you deal and collect the cards in the correct order.

Stage 1 When introducing the animals, remember to line up the four Aces, place the Kings on top of them, the Queens on top of them, and the Jacks on top of them.

Stage 2 When you collect the four piles of cards, hold them face downward and have them cut face downward. When you deal them out into four new piles deal them face downward and go from left to right.

Extra stage If the trick goes well, you might like to add a little bit extra at the end of the trick, by saying that when the zoo-keeper had put the animals into separate cages he stupidly forgot to lock the cages and all the animals escaped and got muddled up again. At this point gather the four piles in your hand, face downward, cut them, deal them into four new piles, still face downward, then turn them up and you will find you now have four piles, with an Ace, a King, a Queen, and a Knave in each!

Coining it!

Equipment: 1 coin

The trick: To perform this trick I need the kind assistance of a member of the audience. Would you please step this way, madam?

Now all I'm going to do is to tap you on the shoulder with one hand and produce a coin from your ear with the other. Hey presto! I've done it.

Now I'm going to tap you on one knee and produce a coin from behind your other knee. Hey presto! I've done it again.

This time I'm going to tap you on the foot and produce a coin from the back of your neck. Hey presto! I've done it once more!

The secret: The secret of this trick — and of any other trick in which you produce a coin from nowhere — is knowing how to *palm* a coin.

Begin by pressing a small coin into the palm of your hand. Press it in really hard. Now lower the fleshy part of your hand under your thumb over the edge of the coin and try holding the coin in position. At first it won't be easy, but with constant practice you should be able to hold the coin in your palm without difficulty.

When holding a coin in the palm of your hand, don't hold your hand open stiffly because it will then be obvious to the audience that it is not in a natural position. Hold your hand slightly closed and, while the coin is hidden in your palm, use the hand quite normally. When you want to produce the coin, simply relax the muscle in your hand and catch the coin in your fingers.

Once you have mastered the art of palming a coin,

you can produce it from absolutely anywhere — from an ear, a knee, the back of the neck!

Dollar power

Equipment: 1 dollar bill

The trick: Is there anyone in the audience lucky enough to have a dollar bill on them?

Ah, good. Would you hold up the dollar sir, so that everybody can see it?

Now crumple the dollar into a tiny little ball and kindly throw it to me. Thank you.

Now I shall throw it to another member of the audience. Are you a good catch, madam? You've got it, well done.

Now, madam, would you unfold the dollar and take a close look at the serial number. Would I be right in thinking that the number is A 46737618 A?

I'm right? Well, I'm not surprised!

The secret: You have a second dollar bill already crumpled up and hidden in your palm before the trick begins. You have memorized the serial number of this dollar bill.

Hold the secret dollar bill in your palm. This takes practice, but if you can palm a coin, you should be able to palm a bill as well! When the first member of the audience throws you his bill catch it in both hands, but throw *your* bill to the second member of the audience with one hand, while pocketing the other dollar bill. The audience will be busy watching you throwing the bill and won't notice you putting your hand into your pocket if you do it naturally.

The serial number you announce is, of course, the number on the bill you have thrown to the second member of the audience. And to make the trick more convincing you can pretend to be having a terrible time trying to think of the serial number, struggling to get it right, and making one or two mistakes along the way!

Meet my amazing assistant!

Equipment: 1 pack of cards
               1 blindfold

The trick: Ladies and gentlemen, I would like you all to meet my amazing assistant. My assistant has the most extraordinary magical powers, as I shall now demonstrate to you.

First of all, I would like a member of the audience to come up on stage and inspect this pack of cards. Would you go through the pack please and remove all the cards of a value less than seven? Thank you. Now would you tie the blindfold around my assistant's eyes? Make sure my assistant cannot see. And make doubly sure by turning my assistant's face away from us.

There are now thirty-two cards left in the pack. Would you pick one out for me? Thank you.

You will agree there is no way my assistant could know what card you have chosen. My assistant certainly can't see it. But I promise you that this amazing assistant of mine will now tell us what the card is.

Now, O amazing assistant, clear your mind. Try to picture the card I'm holding in my hand. Good. Tell me what it is.

"The King of Hearts!"

The secret: You have a code, known only by you and your amazing assistant, and by using the code you can tell him or her exactly what card you are holding, without anybody realizing it. It's a very clever code, difficult to remember and almost impossible to crack. Here it is:

"Now" means it must be a red card.

"Really concentrate" means it must be a black card.

"Clear your mind" means it's either Hearts or Clubs.

"This isn't easy" means it's either Diamonds or Spades."

"Picture the card" means it's either an Ace, a King, a Queen, or a Jack.

"Is it coming?" means it's either a Ten, a Nine, an Eight, or a Seven.

"Fine" means it must be the Ten or the Ace.

"Good" means it must be the Nine or the King.

"Excellent" means it must be the Eight or the Queen.

"Splendid" means it must be the Seven or the Jack.

So that when you say to your assistant, "Now, clear your mind . . . picture the card . . . Good" he knows immediately that the card is the King of Hearts.

Learning the code isn't easy and using it without sounding awkward isn't easy either, but it's well worth working at, because this is one of the most mystifying of all tricks.

P.S. A challenge to keep up your sleeve

SO YOU THINK YOU'RE SO SMART, DO YOU?

In every audience you will come across some smarty-pants, some loud-mouthed know-it-all, who tells everyone that they know exactly how all your tricks are done — and can do several that are a lot better!

Don't worry. That person is no doubt a liar. The more noise they make, the less the rest of the audience will like *them,* and the more the audience will like *you.* However, if they make a real nuisance of themselves, and call out show-stopping remarks like, "I saw how you did that one!" and "That trick's *so easy!*" you will have to deal with them somehow, or they may spoil the show.

The best way is to invite them up onto the stage and say, "If you think you're so smart, I've got a small challenge for you. Since you know so much about magic, I'm sure you will find this very easy, but just to encourage you a bit I will give you a dollar if you can do what I ask!"

Now place a stool against a wall and ask them to face it, standing with their feet together and their toes at a distance about twice the width of the stool away from the wall.

Tell them to bend forward and take hold of both sides of the stool while resting their head against the wall. Now ask them to lift the stool off the floor and stand upright. They simply won't be able to do it! However much you tease and taunt, however much money you offer, they will find it quite impossible — and you can be sure that when they have given up they will return to their seat with a much less swollen head on top of their shoulders!

The Greatest Magic Show on Earth

Once you have practiced all your tricks and mastered all your patter, you will be ready to present The Greatest Magic Show on Earth! Of course, it will only be the *greatest* if you really have perfected your performance with a lot of practice and planned your program with special care.

Always start your show with one of your best tricks and make sure it is one of the ones you feel most confident doing. Always end your show with your most effective and impressive trick. In the middle, perform a number of tricks that show off your skills as a magician. Give the show plenty of variety, be sure to keep it moving, and don't let it go on too long. Don't let your audience get restless and bored. Give them a short show they'll remember and leave them wanting more.

Fifteen minutes is quite long enough for your magic show to last, which means that you will have time to perform seven or eight tricks. In time, you will want to work out a special program for yourself, but to give you an idea of the sort of variety a good magic show needs, here are three different programs, any one of which will give you an exciting quarter-of-an-hour of first class entertainment.

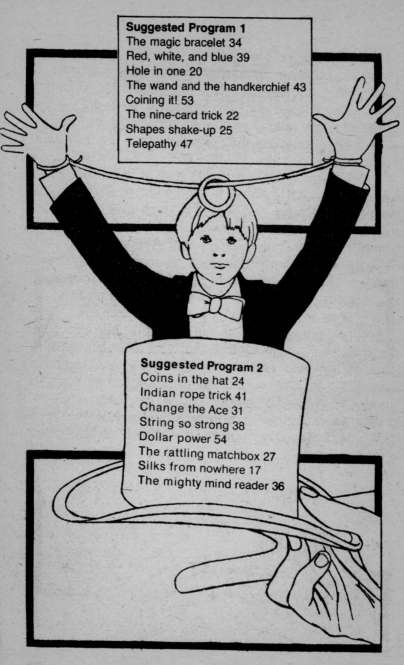

Suggested Program 1
The magic bracelet 34
Red, white, and blue 39
Hole in one 20
The wand and the handkerchief 43
Coining it! 53
The nine-card trick 22
Shapes shake-up 25
Telepathy 47

Suggested Program 2
Coins in the hat 24
Indian rope trick 41
Change the Ace 31
String so strong 38
Dollar power 54
The rattling matchbox 27
Silks from nowhere 17
The mighty mind reader 36

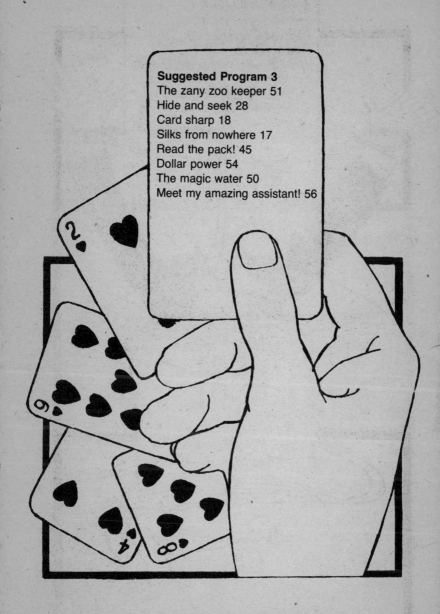

Suggested Program 3
The zany zoo keeper 51
Hide and seek 28
Card sharp 18
Silks from nowhere 17
Read the pack! 45
Dollar power 54
The magic water 50
Meet my amazing assistant! 56